Prehistoric
Record Breakers

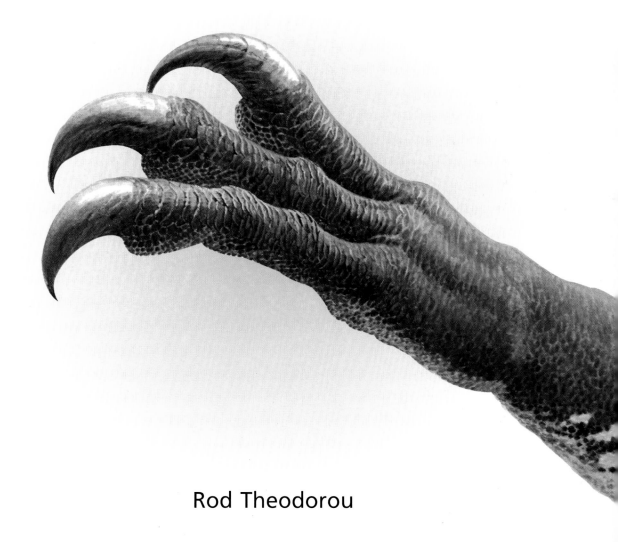

Rod Theodorou

Photo Credits
Rupert Horrox, photography, pages 4, 11, 17, 20 and 21.
Bruce Coleman Limited/Hans Reinhard, page 7.
J Allan Cash Limited, page 9.
Dr Alan Beaumont, page 13.
Ardea/Clem Haagner, page 19.
Bruce Coleman Limited/Uwe Walz, page 22.

Illustrations
James Field/Simon Girling Associates, pages 2, 5, 7, 9, 11, 15, 17, 19, 24 and cover.
Andrew Hutchinson/Illustration, pages 1, 4, 13, 20, 21, 22, 23.
Oxford Illustrators, pages 6, 8, 10, 12, 14, 16, 18.

Discovery World:
Prehistoric Record Breakers

©1998 Rigby

a division of Reed Elsevier Inc.

500 Coventry Lane

Crystal Lake, IL 60014

02 01 00
10 9 8 7 6 5

Printed in the United States of America
ISBN 0-7635-2357-7

Contents

Rigby

About This Book

Prehistoric animals died millions of years ago. Prehistoric animals included dinosaurs, reptiles, and insects.

Have you ever wondered what they were like?

In this book you will find

- information about some of the record-breaking prehistoric animals

- pictures of what these prehistoric animals might have looked like

- guides to help you pronounce each prehistoric animal name

- measurements and scale diagrams of the prehistoric animals

Smallest Dinosaur

🌿 **Name:** Compsognathus

🌿 **Pronounced:** Komp-sog-nay-thus

🌿 **Size:** 30 inches long

Compsognathus is the smallest dinosaur ever to have been discovered. It was a meat-eater. It had long legs and could run fast. It ran fast to catch lizards and insects to eat.

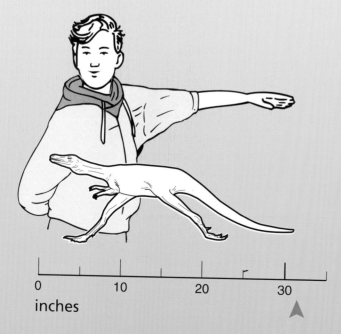

0	10	20	30

inches

Compsognathus was about the
size of a chicken.

Largest Dinosaur

Name: Argentinosaurus

Pronounced: Ar-jen-teen-oh-sore-us

Size: 37 yards long

Some scientists think that Argentinosaurus is the largest and heaviest dinosaur ever to have been discovered. Only a few bones of this massive plant-eater have been found. Argentinosaurus may have weighed more than 12 elephants!

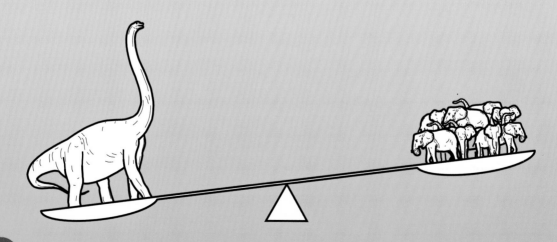

Argentinosaurus was as large as a three-story building.

Largest Meat-eating Dinosaur

Name: Giganotosaurus

Pronounced: Jie-gan-oh-toh-sore-us

Size: 15 yards long

Giganotosaurus is the biggest meat-eating land animal ever to have lived. This predator was even bigger than Tyrannosaurus rex! It was as long as four cars.

Giganotosaurus

Tyrannosaurus rex

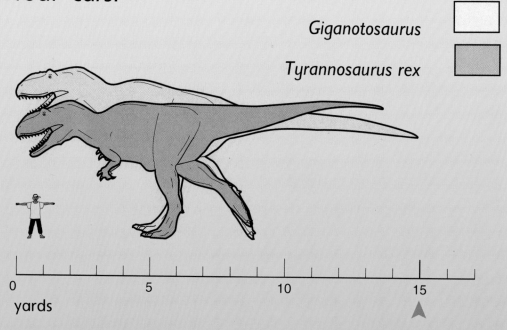

```
0          5          10         15
yards
```

Giganotosaurus had teeth 6 inches long!

Largest Flying Reptile

- **Name:** Quetzalcoatlus
- **Pronounced:** Kwet-zal-co-at-lus
- **Size:** 13 yard wingspan

Quetzalcoatlus is the largest flying creature ever to have lived. Its head was bigger than a whole person! Some scientists think it lived like a giant vulture, eating the bodies of dead dinosaurs.

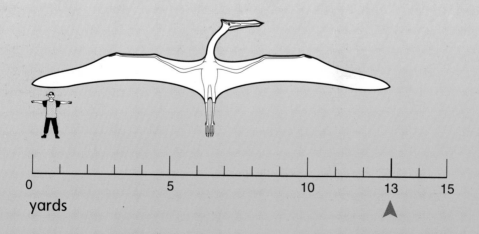

| 0 | | | | | 5 | | | | 10 | | | 13 | 15 |

yards

The wingspan of Quetzalcoatlus was longer than the wingspan of a small plane!

Largest Marine Reptile

- **Name:** Kronosaurus

- **Pronounced:** Kron-oh-sore-us

- **Size:** Over 16 yards long

Kronosaurus is the largest marine or swimming reptile ever to have been discovered. Its head was twice the length of Giganotosaurus' head. Inside its huge mouth were 80 massive teeth. It used these to crush giant turtles and other prey.

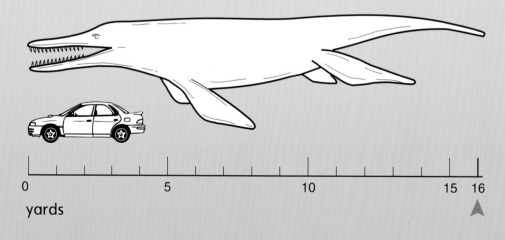

0   5   10   15 16

yards

Kronosaurus was as big as a whale.

Largest Insect

- **Name:** Meganeura
- **Pronounced:** Meg-ah-new-ra
- **Size:** 27 inch wingspan

Meganeura is the largest insect ever to have lived. It was a huge dragonfly that hunted other large insects and small lizards. It may have hovered just like dragonflies do today.

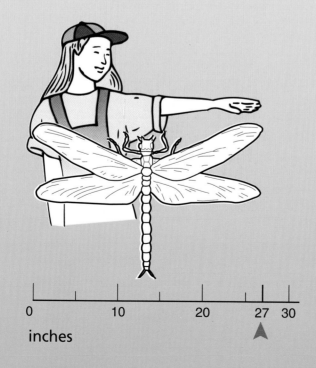

0   10   20   27 30

inches

Meganeura must have made a very loud buzzing noise as it flew!

Fastest Dinosaur

Name: Struthiomimus

Pronounced: Strew-thee-oh-mie-mus

Speed: About 45 miles an hour

Many scientists think Struthiomimus was the fastest dinosaur ever to have lived. It had big, strong legs with huge muscles. These helped it to run away from predators. It ate leaves, insects, and small animals.

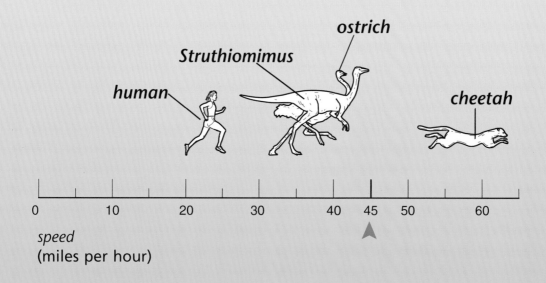

human   Struthiomimus   ostrich   cheetah

| 0 | 10 | 20 | 30 | 40 | 45 | 50 | 60 |

speed
(miles per hour)

Struthiomimus looked like an ostrich but was probably a faster runner.

Longest Arms

- **Name:** Deinocheirus

- **Pronounced:** Dine-oh-kire-us

- **Arm size:** Over 13 feet long

Deinocheirus had the longest arms of any dinosaur. We do not know what Deinocheirus looked like because only the fossil arm bones have been found. They were five times longer than an adult human's arm!

Deinocheirus must have been a huge predator!

Largest Claws

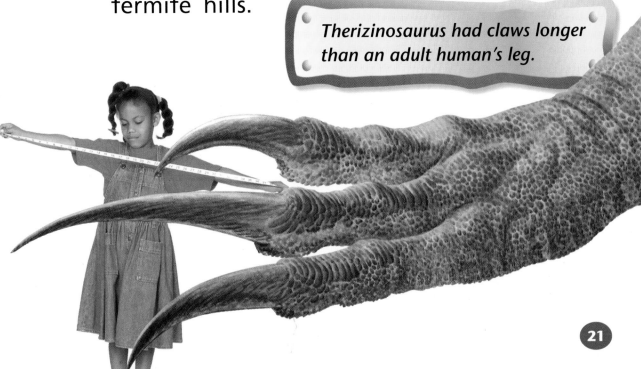

- **Name:** Therizinosaurus
- **Pronounced:** Theh-ree-zin-oh-sore-us
- **Claw size:** About 3 feet long

Therizinosaurus had the largest claws of any dinosaur. Only the fossil claws and a few other small bones have been found. Some scientists think that the large claws were used to dig into termite hills.

Therizinosaurus had claws longer than an adult human's leg.

Largest Head

- **Name:** Torosaurus
- **Pronounced:** Tor-oh-sore-us
- **Head size:** About 10 feet long

Torosaurus had the largest head of any land animal ever to have lived. It was about as long as a family car! It may have used its huge head and sharp horns to scare off enemies.

Torosaurus had a head as big as a whole rhino!

Glossary

fossil

the remains of a living thing
that has turned to stone

predator

an animal that hunts and eats other
animals

prey

an animal that is hunted and eaten by
other animals

scale diagram

a drawing that shows the size of
something

wingspan

the length of an animal from the tip of
one wing to the tip of the other wing

a
b
c
d
e
f
g
h
i
j
k
l
m
n
o
p
q
r
s
t
u
v
w
x
y
z

Index